Autocomplete

Autocomplete: The Book

Justin Hook

CHRONICLE BOOKS
SAN FRANCISCO

Library of Congress Cataloging-in-Publication Data available.

ISBN 978-1-4521-7761-8

Manufactured in China.

Design by Maggie Edelman
Illustrations by Chris Cerrato

1 0 9 8 7 6 5 4 3 2 1

Chronicle Books LLC
680 Second Street
San Francisco, CA 94107
www.chroniclebooks.com

Introduction

For many years, autocomplete couldn't do much more than suggest a recently visited URL or a lengthy word from the dictionary. But in the mid-2000s, search engines began employing it to suggest queries based not only on your past searches, but on those of millions of users around the world. The results were, in almost equal measure, extremely useful and completely bonkers.

I began collecting my favorite autocomplete suggestions, and in 2013, I turned them into an online game called *Google Feud*. Since then it has been played over 100 million times, lampooned on *The Tonight Show*, and declared "your new addiction" by *TIME*. This book features some of my favorite searches from *Google Feud* (updated to the present day), as well as many brand new ones. Some are funny, some are sad, most are weird, and all of them are real.

I hope you recognize some of your own deranged search history in these pages. And if not, what are you waiting for? If you're worried you're going to end up on some kind of list, rest assured that I'm on it, too.

i am extremely terrified

i am extremely terrified **of google**
i am extremely terrified **of flying**
i am extremely terrified **of zombies**
i am extremely terrified **of spiders**

why is it fun to

why is it fun to **stay at the ymca**
why is it fun to **play soccer**
why is it fun to **be drunk**
why is it fun to **travel**
why is it fun to **break things**
why is it fun to **be mean**
why is it fun to **learn a new language**
why is it fun to **be a child**
why is it fun to **pop pimples**
why is it fun to **be scared**

i wish i were a

i wish i were a **bar of soap**
i wish i were a **bird**
i wish i were a **fish**
i wish i were a **little bit taller**
i wish i were a **butterfly**
i wish i were a **girl**
i wish i were a **princess**
i wish i were a **carrot**
i wish i were a **boy**
i wish i were a **unicorn**

giraffes are

giraffes are **heartless creatures**
giraffes are **gay**
giraffes are **fake**
giraffes are **selfish**
giraffes are **dumb**
giraffes are **insincere**
giraffes are **going extinct**
giraffes are **endangered**
giraffes are **cool**
giraffes are **awesome**

can dogs learn to

can dogs learn to **fly**
can dogs learn to **speak**
can dogs learn to **read**
can dogs learn to **drive**
can dogs learn to **use a litter box**
can dogs learn to **smile**
can dogs learn to **count**
can dogs learn to **understand english**
can dogs learn to **use the toilet**
can dogs learn to **get along**

what's the secret of

what's the secret of **life**
what's the secret of **sokolowski's staying power**
what's the secret of **happiness**
what's the secret of **victoria's secret**
what's the secret of **bleak falls barrow**
what's the secret of **oak island**
what's the secret of **a happy relationship**
what's the secret of **success**
what's the secret of **living a long life**
what's the secret of **the krabby patty formula**

is there such thing as a

is there such thing as a **sugar high**
is there such thing as a **million dollar bill**
is there such thing as a **$1000 bill**
is there such thing as a **mini pig**
is there such thing as a **black panther**
is there such thing as a **blue moon**
is there such thing as a **liger**
is there such thing as a **snow snake**
is there such thing as a **5.0 gpa**
is there such thing as a **perfect circle**

do all celebrities have

do all celebrities have personal assistants

do all celebrities have **herpes**

do all celebrities have **plastic surgery**

do all celebrities have **veneers**

do all celebrities have **to join the illuminati**

do all celebrities have **iphones**

do all celebrities have **to sell their souls**

do all celebrities have **bodyguards**

do all celebrities have **agents**

do all celebrities have **nannies**

can i name my baby

can i name my baby **jesus**
can i name my baby **hitler**
can i name my baby **lucifer**
can i name my baby **anything**
can i name my baby **god**
can i name my baby **a different last name**
can i name my baby **baby**
can i name my baby **beyonce**
can i name my baby **blue ivy**
can i name my baby **king**

my son wants to be

my son wants to be **a youtuber**
my son wants to be **homeless**
my son wants to be **a professional gamer**
my son wants to be **a marine**
my son wants to be **a girl**
my son wants to be **a rapper**
my son wants to be **a baby again**
my son wants to be **a professional soccer player**
my son wants to be **an architect**
my son wants to be **a ballerina**

my daughter wants to be

my daughter wants to be **a man**
my daughter wants to be **a baby**
my daughter wants to be **an actress**
my daughter wants to be **a doctor**
my daughter wants to be **a surgeon**
my daughter wants to be **a model**
my daughter wants to be **a cheerleader**
my daughter wants to be **a nun**
my daughter wants to be **a singer**
my daughter wants to be **homeless**

what happens if you put a

what happens if you put a **car in park while driving**
what happens if you put a **garlic clove in your ear**
what happens if you put a **tide pod in your mouth**
what happens if you put a **battery in water**
what happens if you put a **tampon in wrong**
what happens if you put a **muffler on backwards**
what happens if you put a **spoon in a microwave**
what happens if you put a **fork in a toaster**
what happens if you put a **saltwater fish in freshwater**
what happens if you put a **light bulb in your mouth**

i can't figure out how to

i can't figure out how to **turn my shower on**
i can't figure out how to **make money**
i can't figure out how to **curl my hair**
i can't figure out how to **put a tampon in**
i can't figure out how to **do kegels**
i can't figure out how to **tie a tie**
i can't figure out how to **crochet**
i can't figure out how to **curl my hair with a straightener**
i can't figure out how to **delete my twitter**
i can't figure out how to **do a cartwheel**

were the 90s

were the 90s **the best decade**
were the 90s **better than now**
were the 90s **conservative**
were the 90s **the last great decade**
were the 90s **really that great**
were the 90s **a simpler time**
were the 90s **that great**
were the 90s **a long time ago**
were the 90s **a happier time**

new york is full of

new york is full of **snobs**

la is full of

la is full of **douchebags**

why don't fish

why don't fish **drown**
why don't fish **blink**
why don't fish **feel pain**
why don't fish **sink**
why don't fish **float**
why don't fish **and cheese go together**
why don't fish **have legs**
why don't fish **have hair**
why don't fish **play basketball**
why don't fish **have fat**

is my bird

is my bird **gay**
is my bird **a terrorist**
is my bird **dead**
is my bird **sick**
is my bird **choking**
is my bird **egg bound**
is my bird **dying**
is my bird **molting**
is my bird **lonely**
is my bird **cold**

can the government control

can the government control **the internet**
can the government control **your phone**
can the government control **earthquakes**
can the government control **the rain**
can the government control **the weather**
can the government control **your car**
can the government control **your computer**
can the government control **the media**
can the government control **your dreams**
can the government control **cryptocurrency**

is it too late for me to become

is it too late for me to become **a doctor**
is it too late for me to become **a nurse**
is it too late for me to become **an actor**
is it too late for me to become **an olympic athlete**
is it too late for me to become **a lawyer**
is it too late for me to become **a dancer**
is it too late for me to become **a pro soccer player**
is it too late for me to become **an engineer**
is it too late for me to become **an astronaut**
is it too late for me to become **a vet**

why aren't there any

why aren't there any **b batteries**
why aren't there any **cures for genetic disorders**
why aren't there any **nhl players in the olympics**
why aren't there any **green stars**
why aren't there any **snakes in ireland**
why aren't there any **narwhals in captivity**
why aren't there any **dwarves in lord of the rings**
why aren't there any **purple flags**
why aren't there any **female navy seals**
why aren't there any **girl minions**

can you die from eating too much

can you die from eating too much **chocolate**
can you die from eating too much **sugar**
can you die from eating too much **salt**
can you die from eating too much **weed**
can you die from eating too much **chicken nuggets**
can you die from eating too much **spicy food**
can you die from eating too much **ice**
can you die from eating too much **cheese**
can you die from eating too much **pizza**
can you die from eating too much **candy**

seafood makes me

seafood makes me **nauseous**
seafood makes me **poop**
seafood makes me **fart**
seafood makes me **sleepy**
seafood makes me **gag**
seafood makes me **gassy**
seafood makes me **smell**
seafood makes me **sick**
seafood makes me **itchy**
seafood makes me **pregnant**

why do millennials

why do millennials **job hop**
why do millennials **travel**
why do millennials **eat tide pods**
why do millennials **love avocados**
why do millennials **love nostalgia**
why do millennials **talk so fast**
why do millennials **not vote**
why do millennials **rent**
why do millennials **swear so much**
why do millennials **like bernie**

millennials are killing

millennials are killing **diamonds**
millennials are killing **lunch**
millennials are killing **reddit**
millennials are killing **collage**
millennials are killing **golf**
millennials are killing **cereal**
millennials are killing **napkins**
millennials are killing **chains**
millennials are killing **marriage**
millennials are killing **capitalism**

i want to buy a

i want to buy a **house**
i want to buy a **timeshare**
i want to buy a **car**
i want to buy a **star**
i want to buy a **horse**
i want to buy a **tiny house**
i want to buy a **puppy**
i want to buy a **boat**
i want to buy a **gun**
i want to buy a **bitcoin**

where can you sell a

where can you sell a **testicle**
where can you sell a **gun**
where can you sell a **laptop**
where can you sell a **diamond**
where can you sell a **fur coat**
where can you sell a **phone**
where can you sell a **wedding dress**
where can you sell a **dog**
where can you sell a **stamp collection**
where can you sell a **computer**

is it fun to be a

is it fun to be a **girl**
is it fun to be a **cat**
is it fun to be a **boy**
is it fun to be a **lawyer**
is it fun to be a **teacher**
is it fun to be a **doctor**
is it fun to be a **cop**
is it fun to be a **pet named steve**
is it fun to be a **pilot**
is it fun to be a **surgeon**

my armpits smell like

my armpits smell like **curry**

my armpits smell like **cat pee**

my armpits smell like **garlic**

my armpits smell like **cheese**

my armpits smell like **yeast**

my armpits smell like **fish**

my armpits smell like **vinegar**

my armpits smell like **onions**

my armpits smell like **tacos**

my armpits smell like **crayons**

why do they still make

why do they still make **pennies**
why do they still make **music videos**
why do they still make **manual cars**
why do they still make **$2 bills**
why do they still make **flat head screws**
why do they still make **cds**
why do they still make **ipods**
why do they still make **black jelly beans**
why do they still make **phone books**
why do they still make **dvds**

will i get caught

will i get caught **driving without a license**
will i get caught **plagiarizing**
will i get caught **buying drugs online**
will i get caught **lying on my taxes**
will i get caught **hit and run**
will i get caught **torrenting**
will i get caught **for hitting a parked car**
will i get caught **shoplifting**
will i get caught **stealing from work**
will i get caught **not paying tax**

is my grandmother

is my grandmother **haunting me**

does anyone else hate

does anyone else hate **christmas**
does anyone else hate **windows 10**
does anyone else hate **facebook**
does anyone else hate **rory gilmore**
does anyone else hate **being pregnant**
does anyone else hate **football**
does anyone else hate **dogs**
does anyone else hate **meredith grey**
does anyone else hate **google feud**
does anyone else hate **their birthday**

does anyone else like

does anyone else like **soggy cereal**
does anyone else like **being alone**
does anyone else like **the smell of their own farts**
does anyone else like **the smell of period blood**
does anyone else like **the feeling of pooping**
does anyone else like **the smell of their own balls**
does anyone else like **stale marshmallows**
does anyone else like **popping pimples**
does anyone else like **the smell of gasoline**
does anyone else like **flat soda**

i'm in love with my

i'm in love with my **best friend**
i'm in love with my **car**
i'm in love with my **sadness**
i'm in love with my **friend**
i'm in love with my **ex**
i'm in love with my **life**
i'm in love with my **sister**
i'm in love with my **boyfriend**
i'm in love with my **boss**
i'm in love with my **cousin**

how to kiss someone with

how to kiss someone with **braces**

how to kiss someone with **a beard**

how to kiss someone with **a big nose**

how to kiss someone with **glasses**

how to kiss someone with **a small mouth**

how to kiss someone with **small lips**

how to kiss someone with **a lip ring**

how to kiss someone with**out them knowing**

how to kiss someone with **tongue**

how to kiss someone with **mono and not get it**

is it ok to

is it ok to **be white**
is it ok to **swallow gum**
is it ok to **eat snow**
is it ok to **run everyday**
is it ok to **give cats milk**
is it ok to **freeze cheese**
is it ok to **drink distilled water**
is it ok to **eat raw eggs**
is it ok to **workout when sick**
is it ok to **start a sentence with and**

my friend is a

my friend is a **one upper**
my friend is a **bridezilla**
my friend is a **freeloader**
my friend is a **therapist**
my friend is a **creeper**
my friend is a **compulsive liar**
my friend is a **pathological liar**
my friend is a **bad parent**
my friend is a **pain in the neck**
my friend is a **communist**

my best friend is a

my best friend is a **guy**
my best friend is a **monkey**
my best friend is a **girl**
my best friend is a **bag**
my best friend is a **marine**
my best friend is a **mermaid**
my best friend is a **robot**
my best friend is a **dog**
my best friend is a **cat**
my best friend is a **secret agent**

can a vagina

can a vagina **have teeth**
can a vagina **fall out**

can a penis

can a penis **shrink**
can a penis **be enlarged**
can a penis **fall off**

has a dog ever been

has a dog ever been **gay**
has a dog ever been **bred with a cat**
has a dog ever been **knighted**
has a dog ever been **to space**
has a dog ever been **mayor**
has a dog ever been **nominated for an oscar**
has a dog ever been **cloned**
has a dog ever been **attacked by a shark**
has a dog ever been **struck by lightning**
has a dog ever been **awarded the medal of honor**

should i stop

should i stop **drinking**
should i stop **masturbating**
should i stop **smoking weed**
should i stop **drinking coffee**
should i stop **texting her**
should i stop **eating meat**
should i stop **taking creatine**
should i stop **talking to him**
should i stop **playing video games**
should i stop **eating bread**

does anyone else eat

does anyone else eat **dry ramen noodles**
does anyone else eat **their discharge**
does anyone else eat **their skin**
does anyone else eat **nutella out of the jar**
does anyone else eat **their boogers**
does anyone else eat **their scabs**
does anyone else eat **raw ramen noodles**
does anyone else eat **baby food**
does anyone else eat **raw pasta**
does anyone else eat **peanut shells**

why is my son so

why is my son so **angry**

why is my son so **pale**

why is my son so **tired**

why is my son so **weird**

why is my son so **lazy**

why is my son so **skinny**

why is my son so **attached to me**

why is my son so **loud**

why is my son so **sensitive**

why is my son so **gassy**

why is my daughter so

why is my daughter so **mean**

why is my daughter so **pale**

why is my daughter so **beautiful**

why is my daughter so **crazy**

why is my daughter so **cute**

why is my daughter so **angry**

why is my daughter so **attached to me**

why is my daughter so **lazy**

why is my daughter so **tired**

why is my daughter so **shy**

why isn't the world

why isn't the world **covered in poop**

why isn't the world **one country**

why isn't the world **peaceful**

why isn't the world **perfect**

why isn't the world **map upside down**

why isn't the world **inundated with bacteria**

why isn't the world **fair**

why isn't the world **covered in bacteria**

why isn't the world **doing anything about syria**

why isn't the world **map to scale**

why is it ok for

why is it ok for **hockey players to fight**
why is it ok for **god to be jealous**
why is it ok for **animals to eat animals**
why is it ok for **sacral vertebrae to be fused**
why is it ok for **guys to be shirtless**
why is it ok for **us to have nuclear weapons**
why is it ok for **doctors to make you wait**
why is it ok for **vegetarians to eat fish**
why is it ok for **israel to have nuclear weapons**
why is it ok for **diplomats to lie**

how to be more like

how to be more like **jesus**
how to be more like **a girl**
how to be more like **mr rogers**
how to be more like **sherlock holmes**
how to be more like **ron swanson**
how to be more like **a woman**
how to be more like **don draper**
how to be more like **james bond**
how to be more like **yourself**
how to be more like **beyonce**

i want to steal a

i want to steal a **kiss**
i want to steal a **dog**
i want to steal a **girl from her boyfriend**
i want to steal a **donut truck**
i want to steal a **married man**
i want to steal a **baby**
i want to steal a **car**
i want to steal a **phone**
i want to steal a **cat**
i want to steal a **bike**

can you pet a

can you pet a **fish**

can you pet a **service dog**

can you pet a **porcupine**

can you pet a **fox**

can you pet a **betta fish**

can you pet a **wild possum**

can you pet a **hummingbird**

can you pet a **seal**

can you pet a **penguin**

can you pet a **hedgehog**

should i burn my

should i burn my **ouija board**
should i burn my **lawn**
should i burn my **diary**
should i burn my **leaves**
should i burn my **pasture**
should i burn my **ex letters**
should i burn my **garbage**
should i burn my **ex stuff**
should i burn my **bridges**
should i burn my **christmas tree in the fireplace**

i got scammed by

i got scammed by **a silicon valley startup**
i got scammed by **microsoft**
i got scammed by **a sugar daddy**
i got scammed by **a website**
i got scammed by **opskins**
i got scammed by **an ebay seller**
i got scammed by **bitconnect**
i got scammed by **bank transfer**
i got scammed by **a modeling agency**
i got scammed by **a psychic**

help my daughter is

help my daughter is **cutting herself**

help my daughter is **dating a loser**

help my daughter is **obese**

help my daughter is **being bullied**

help my daughter is **a mean girl**

help my daughter is **out of control**

help my daughter is **an atheist**

help my daughter is **in jail**

help my daughter is **sexting**

help my daughter is **transgender**

help my son is

help my son is **a furry**
help my son is **suicidal**
help my son is **on drugs**
help my son is **out of control**
help my son is **a communist**
help my son is **transgender**
help my son is **failing high school**
help my son is **addicted to gaming**
help my son is a **pothead**
help my son is a **leper**

ducks are

ducks are **the best**
ducks are **rapists**
ducks are **awesome**
ducks are **i**n a row
ducks are **birds**
ducks are **like toasters**
ducks are **necrophiliacs**
ducks are **cute**
ducks are **evil**
ducks are **mean**

penguins are

penguins are **gay**
penguins are **birds**
penguins are **panda chickens**
penguins are **evil**
penguins are **so sensitive**
penguins are **jerks**
penguins are **dinosaurs**
penguins are **mammals**
penguins are **awesome**
penguins are **cute**

am i a bad person if i

am i a bad person if i **eat meat**

am i a bad person if i **get an abortion**

am i a bad person if i**'m not vegan**

am i a bad person if i **cheat**

am i a bad person if i **don't like dogs**

am i a bad person if i **smoke weed**

am i a bad person if i **have bpd**

am i a bad person if i **give up my dog**

am i a bad person if i **don't go to a funeral**

am i a bad person if i **get a divorce**

is it bad

is it bad **to crack your back**
is it bad **to swallow gum**
is it bad **that i never made love**
is it bad **to hold in your farts**
is it bad **to smoke weed**
is it bad **to crack your fingers**
is it bad **to eat ice**
is it bad **to sleep with wet hair**
is it bad **to drink cold water**
is it bad **to close a credit card**

is it good to

is it good to **cry**
is it good to **fast**
is it good to **fart**
is it good to **lease a car**
is it good to **sweat**
is it good to **run everyday**
is it good to **be sore**
is it good to **workout at night**
is it good to **brush your hair**
is it good to **eat after workout**

can jesus

can jesus **microwave a burrito**
can jesus **fly**
can jesus **cure cancer**
can jesus **heal**
can jesus **be god**
can jesus **heal cancer**
can jesus **speak english**
can jesus **talk to you**
can jesus **sing**
can jesus **come at any time**

should i tell my mom

should i tell my mom **i smoke weed**
should i tell my mom **i'm having an abortion**
should i tell my mom **i'm pregnant**
should i tell my mom **i have a boyfriend**
should i tell my mom **the truth**
should i tell my mom **that i lost my virginity**
should i tell my mom **about my abortion**
should i tell my mom **i smoke**
should i tell my mom **i have a uti**
should i tell my mom **i hate her**

should i tell my dad

should i tell my dad **he has dementia**
should i tell my dad **i smoke weed**
should i tell my dad **my mom is cheating on him**
should i tell my dad **i'm sexually attracted to him**
should i tell my dad **i got my period**
should i tell my dad **about my boyfriend**
should i tell my dad **he is dying**
should i tell my dad **he has cancer**
should i tell my dad **i'm gay**
should i tell my dad **happy fathers day**

my friend is addicted to

my friend is addicted to **weed**
my friend is addicted to **her phone**
my friend is addicted to **google feud**
my friend is addicted to **fortnite**
my friend is addicted to **adderall**
my friend is addicted to **coke**
my friend is addicted to **drugs**
my friend is addicted to **vaping**
my friend is addicted to **league of legends**
my friend is addicted to **instagram**

will i die if i

will i die if i **get the flu**
will i die if i **swallow gum**
will i die if i **shotgun a four loko**
will i die if i **have hiv**
will i die if i **eat mold**
will i die if i **eat poop**
will i die if i **smoke weed**
will i die if i **eat lettuce**
will i die if i **drink a gallon of water**
will i die if i **join the military**

i'm sad about

i'm sad about **my life**
i'm sad about **moving out**
i'm sad about **graduating high school**
i'm sad about **my ex**
i'm sad about **my break up**
i'm sad about **leaving high school**
i'm sad about **growing up**
i'm sad about **leaving for college**
i'm sad about **turning 20**
i'm sad about **a boy**

how do i make myself look

how do i make myself look **older**
how do i make myself look **pretty**
how do i make myself look **younger**
how do i make myself look **sick**
how do i make myself look **skinnier**
how do i make myself look **beautiful**
how do i make myself look **more feminine**
how do i make myself look **more masculine**
how do i make myself look **slimmer in a photo**
how do i make myself look **offline on messenger**

is 10 a good age to

is 10 a good age to **get a cell phone**
is 10 a good age to **start dating**
is 10 a good age to **wear makeup**
is 10 a good age to **start gymnastics**
is 10 a good age to **start shaving**
is 10 a good age to **get a phone**

is 20 a good age to

is 20 a good age to **get married**
is 20 a good age to **get pregnant**
is 20 a good age to **start boxing**
is 20 a good age to **move out**
is 20 a good age to **lose your virginity**
is 20 a good age to **join the military**
is 20 a good age to **start acting**
is 20 a good age to **start dating**
is 20 a good age to **get a boyfriend**
is 20 a good age to **have a baby**

is 30 a good age to

is 30 a good age to **have a baby**
is 30 a good age to **get married**
is 30 a good age to **die**
is 30 a good age to **start a family**
is 30 a good age to **buy a house**

is 40 a good age to

is 40 a good age to **have a baby**
is 40 a good age to **get married**
is 40 a good age to **be a dad**

is 50 a good age to

is 50 a good age to **retire**
is 50 a good age to **die**

is 60 a good age to

is 60 a good age to **retire**
is 60 a good age to **die**

is 70 a good age to

is 70 a good age to **die**

is 80 a good age to

is 80 a good age to **die**

is 90 a good age to

is 90 a good age to **live to**

is 100 a good age to

does santa claus have

does santa claus have **a son**
does santa claus have **a birthday**
does santa claus have **diabetes**
does santa claus have **a brother**
does santa claus have **a pilot's license**
does santa claus have **a phone**
does santa claus have **a dog**
does santa claus have **a middle name**
does santa claus have **an e**
does santa claus have **hair**

i wasted my

i wasted my **life**
i wasted my **20s**
i wasted my **time**
i wasted my **youth**
i wasted my **college years**
i wasted my **childhood**
i wasted my **teenage years**
i wasted my **time on you**
i wasted my **money**
i wasted my **time in college**

i crashed my car into

i crashed my car into **a bridge**
i crashed my car into **a cop car**
i crashed my car into **my house**
i crashed my car into **a tree**
i crashed my car into **a tree trying to kill a bee**
i crashed my car into **a pole**
i crashed my car into **a ditch**
i crashed my car into **a wall**
i crashed my car into **another car**
i crashed my car into **a curb**

will i ever be able to

will i ever be able to **grow a beard**
will i ever be able to **retire**
will i ever be able to **afford a house**
will i ever be able to **love again**
will i ever be able to **eat gluten again**
will i ever be able to **dunk**
will i ever be able to **sing**
will i ever be able to **do a push up**
will i ever be able to **do a split**
will i ever be able to **lose weight**

from what age can babies

from what age can babies **fly**
from what age can babies **fight to the death**
from what age can babies **drink water**
from what age can babies **have gripe water**
from what age can babies **sit in a bumbo**
from what age can babies **eat**
from what age can babies **see**
from what age can babies **sit**
from what age can babies **eat egg**
from what age can babies **swim**

my uncle is

my uncle is **a marine**

my uncle is **my guardian angel**

my uncle is **my hero**

my uncle is **a firefighter**

my uncle is **a raft**

my uncle is **my dad**

my uncle is **a trains man**

my uncle is **the green river killer**

my uncle is **cooler than yours**

my uncle is **my superhero**

my grandmother is

my grandmother is **a warrior**
my grandmother is **pregnant**
my grandmother is **haunting me**
my grandmother is **dying**
my grandmother is **a bike**
my grandmother is **going to die**
my grandmother is **my role model**
my grandmother is **talking to herself**
my grandmother is **crazy**
my grandmother is **dead**

how to get out of

how to get out of **debt**

how to get out of **jury duty**

how to get out of **a lease**

how to get out of **depression**

how to get out of **a car lease**

how to get out of **credit card debt**

how to get out of **the friend zone**

how to get out of **safe mode**

how to get out of **a car loan**

how to get out of **a funk**

why is it so hard to

why is it so hard to **find a job**
why is it so hard to **lose weight**
why is it so hard to **wake up**
why is it so hard to **quit smoking**
why is it so hard to **find love**
why is it so hard to **make friends**
why is it so hard to **let go**
why is it so hard to **sleep**
why is it so hard to **be happy**
why is it so hard to **poop**

can you eat your own

can you eat your own **poop**
can you eat your own **skin**
can you eat your own **placenta**
can you eat your own **blood**
can you eat your own **hair**
can you eat your own **flesh**
can you eat your own **food on a plane**
can you eat your own **tongue**
can you eat your own **boogers**
can you eat your own **vomit**

i ate an entire

i ate an entire **onion**
i ate an entire **cake**
i ate an entire **watermelon**
i ate an entire **pack of oreos**
i ate an entire **avocado**
i ate an entire **loaf of bread**
i ate an entire **can of pringles**
i ate an entire **jar of pickles**
i ate an entire **chocolate bar**
i ate an entire **bag of goldfish**

i hate the taste of

i hate the taste of **water**
i hate the taste of **weed**
i hate the taste of **beer**
i hate the taste of **whiskey**
i hate the taste of **protein powder**
i hate the taste of **coffee**
i hate the taste of **milk**
i hate the taste of **wine**
i hate the taste of **meat**
i hate the taste of **alcohol**

what happens if you microwave

what happens if you microwave **weed**
what happens if you microwave **metal**
what happens if you microwave **an egg**
what happens if you microwave **dry ice**
what happens if you microwave **an iphone**
what happens if you microwave **styrofoam**
what happens if you microwave **nothing**
what happens if you microwave **fire**
what happens if you microwave **a spoon**
what happens if you microwave **slime**

personally i don't like

personally i don't like **cheesecake**

londoners are

londoners are **unfriendly**
londoners are **rude**
londoners are **arrogant**
londoners are **miserable**
londoners are **boring**
londoners are **cold**
londoners are **nice**
londoners are **friendly**
londoners are **selfish**
londoners are **ignorant**

new yorkers are

new yorkers are **rude**
new yorkers are **annoying**
new yorkers are **idiots**
new yorkers are **known for**
new yorkers are **tough**
new yorkers are **nice**
new yorkers are **friendly**
new yorkers are **stupid**
new yorkers are **arrogant**
new yorkers are **crazy**

i like the taste of

i like the taste of **blood**
i like the taste of **alcohol**
i like the taste of **apple cider vinegar**
i like the taste of **beer**
i like the taste of **water**
i like the taste of **cigarettes**
i like the taste of **rubber bands**
i like the taste of **tums**
i like the taste of **bleach**
i like the taste of **vinegar**

donald trump looks like

donald trump looks like **mussolini**
donald trump looks like **butter**
donald trump looks like **corn**
donald trump looks like **owen wilson**
donald trump looks like **biff**
donald trump looks like **pokemon**
donald trump looks like **dr evil**
donald trump looks like **oompa loompa**
donald trump looks like **donald duck**
donald trump looks like **a pumpkin**

is america

is america **a country**
is america **an island**
is america **a democracy**
is america **capitalist**
is america **at war**
is america **a continent**
is america **an empire**
is america **in debt**
is america **a free country**
is america **communist**

where is it legal to

where is it legal to **own a fox**
where is it legal to **smoke weed**
where is it legal to **own an otter**
where is it legal to **drink at 18**
where is it legal to **own a hedgehog**
where is it legal to **marry your cousin**
where is it legal to **own a wolf**
where is it legal to **sleep in your car**
where is it legal to **own a fennec fox**
where is it legal to **own a tiger**

i was bitten by a

i was bitten by a **turtle**
i was bitten by a **dog**
i was bitten by a **human**
i was bitten by a **black widow**
i was bitten by a **snake**
i was bitten by a **mouse**
i was bitten by a **spider**
i was bitten by a **deer tick**
i was bitten by a **squirrel**
i was bitten by a **cat**

do cats know

do cats know **their names**
do cats know **when they are going to die**
do cats know **when another cat dies**
do cats know **their siblings**
do cats know **they are loved**
do cats know **they are cats**
do cats know **how to swim**
do cats know **when you are pregnant**
do cats know **their owners**
do cats know **what kisses are**

my dog ate my

my dog ate my **homework**
my dog ate my **weed**
my dog ate my **birth control**
my dog ate my **chapstick**
my dog ate my **edibles**
my dog ate my **cat**
my dog ate my **pad**
my dog ate my **glasses**
my dog ate my **poop**
my dog ate my **salad**

should i study or

should i study or **sleep**
should i study or **work**
should i study or **go out**
should i study or **not**
should i study or **watch netflix**
should i study or **play video games**
should i study or **go to sleep**
should i study or **do homework first**
should i study or **watch a movie**
should i study or **workout**

were there really

were there really **pirates**
were there really **300 spartans**
were there really **amazons**
were there really **disappointment rooms**
were there really **handmaids**
were there really **vikings**
were there really **musketeers**
were there really **greek gods**
were there really **cowboys**
were there really **trains in the underground railroad**

how to tell your parents you're

how to tell your parents you're **moving out**
how to tell your parents you're **pregnant**
how to tell your parents you're **moving in with your boyfriend**
how to tell your parents you're **dating someone**
how to tell your parents you're **engaged**
how to tell your parents you're **depressed**
how to tell your parents you're **bi**
how to tell your parents you're **transgender**
how to tell your parents you're **pansexual**
how to tell your parents you're **a furry**

how can you meet

how can you meet **the president**
how can you meet **jojo siwa**
how can you meet **bts**
how can you meet **stephen curry**
how can you meet **lebron james**
how can you meet **the queen of england**
how can you meet **dolly parton**
how can you meet **the pope**
how can you meet **eminem in person**
how can you meet **taylor swift at a concert**

should i allow my son to

should i allow my son to **play fortnite**
should i allow my son to **have a girlfriend**
should i allow my son to **play football**
should i allow my son to **smoke pot**
should i allow my son to **sleep with his girlfriend**
should i allow my son to **quit football**
should i allow my son to **join a fraternity**
should i allow my son to **play gta 5**
should i allow my son to **wear makeup**
should i allow my son to **vape**

should i allow my daughter to

should i allow my daughter to **have snapchat**
should i allow my daughter to **have a boyfriend**
should i allow my daughter to **wear a bikini**
should i allow my daughter to **get snapchat**
should i allow my daughter to **wear thongs**
should i allow my daughter to **wear tampons**
should i allow my daughter to **have instagram**
should i allow my daughter to **smoke**
should i allow my daughter to **shave her pubic hair**
should i allow my daughter to **pierce her nose**

do dogs know

do dogs know **they are dogs**
do dogs know **they are dying**
do dogs know **when you are sad**
do dogs know **time**
do dogs know **you love them**
do dogs know **when your sick**
do dogs know **their name**
do dogs know **when they fart**
do dogs know **they are cute**
do dogs know **calculus**

$x\sqrt{3}$

$\times \sqrt{\text{} \left(1 - \text{}\right)^2}$

$$\int \frac{dx}{\cos^2 x} = tgx + c$$

$= \dfrac{1}{3}\pi r^2 / 2$

$C = 2\pi$

$A = \pi r$

$$\int \sin x \, dx = -\cos x + c$$

why would anyone

why would anyone **need a credit card**

why would anyone **need an assault rifle**

why would anyone **believe in god**

why would anyone **like me**

why would anyone **need an ar 15**

why would anyone **want to use fear in a commercial**

why would anyone **want to be a cop**

why would anyone **work as an unpaid intern**

why would anyone **get married**

why would anyone **want to be president**

am i good enough to

am i good enough to **be a doctor**
am i good enough to **go to heaven**
am i good enough to **play college football**
am i good enough to **be an actress**
am i good enough to **be a singer**
am i good enough to **get into harvard**
am i good enough to **be a writer**
am i good enough to **model**
am i good enough to **date**
am i good enough to **be loved**

can adults go to

can adults go to **legoland**

can adults go to **high school**

can adults go to **trampoline park**

can adults go to **a pediatrician**

can adults go to **college**

can adults go to **disneyland**

can adults go to **chuck e cheese**

can adults go to **work with pink eye**

can adults go to **planned parenthood**

can adults go to **woodward**

i want to marry a

i want to marry a **lighthouse keeper**
i want to marry a **creative jewish girl**
i want to marry a **millionaire**
i want to marry a **doctor**
i want to marry a **british guy**
i want to marry a **foreigner**
i want to marry a **japanese woman**
i want to marry a **prince**
i want to marry a **white man**
i want to marry a **pastor**

am i too old for

am i too old for **tinder**
am i too old for **college**
am i too old for **braces**
am i too old for **law school**
am i too old for **lasik**
am i too old for **hair extensions**
am i too old for **a brazilian wax**
am i too old for **video games**
am i too old for **med school**
am i too old for **overalls**

am i too young for

am i too young for **botox**
am i too young for **a heart attack**
am i too young for **him**
am i too young for **match.com**
am i too young for **viagra**
am i too young for **lasik**
am i too young for **retinol**
am i too young for **gout**
am i too young for **a mammogram**
am i too young for **knee replacement surgery**

i like guys with

i like guys with **spikes**
i like guys with **long hair**
i like guys with **beards**
i like guys with **glasses**
i like guys with **big noses**
i like guys with **big hands**
i like guys with **big bellies**
i like guys with **girlfriends**
i like guys with **acne**
i like guys with **crooked teeth**

why don't people

why don't people **like me**
why don't people **like the last jedi**
why don't people **vote**
why don't people **recycle**
why don't people **talk to me**
why don't people **exercise**
why don't people **eat turkey eggs**
why don't people **listen to me**
why don't people **like change**
why don't people **respect me**

a girl keeps

a girl keeps **staring at me**
a girl keeps **flirting with me**
a girl keeps **sending me selfies**
a girl keeps **talking about me**
a girl keeps **calling me cute**
a girl keeps **playfully hitting me**
a girl keeps **staring at me in class**
a girl keeps **smiling at me**
a girl keeps **glancing at me**

a boy keeps

a boy keeps **teasing me**

a boy keeps **staring at me**

a boy keeps **staring at me in class**

a boy keeps **asking for pictures**

a boy keeps **touching me**

a boy keeps **texting me**

a boy keeps **touching my hair**

a boy keeps **flirting with me**

a boy keeps **smiling at me**

a boy keeps **asking me out**

does anyone else think

does anyone else think **kylo ren is hot**
does anyone else think **life is pointless**
does anyone else think **shrek is hot**
does anyone else think **the beatles are overrated**
does anyone else think **tattoos are stupid**
does anyone else think **like me**
does anyone else think **babies are ugly**
does anyone else think **elsa is hot**
does anyone else think **snape is hot**
does anyone else think **flo is hot**

will i regret

will i regret **not having children**
will i regret **not going to prom**
will i regret **eloping**
will i regret **scalp micropigmentation**
will i regret **not having kids**
will i regret **not having a wedding**
will i regret **an abortion**
will i regret **my divorce**
will i regret **getting bangs**
will i regret **having a child**

i'm only happy when i'm

i'm only happy when i'm **with you**
i'm only happy when i'm **with my boyfriend**
i'm only happy when i'm **in a relationship**
i'm only happy when i'm **high**
i'm only happy when i'm **asleep**
i'm only happy when i'm **distracted**
i'm only happy when i'm **dancing**
i'm only happy when i'm **drunk**
i'm only happy when i'm **with you home for me is where you are**
i'm only happy when i'm **alone**

can you get paid to

can you get paid to **blog**
can you get paid to **sleep**
can you get paid to **go to college**
can you get paid to **donate sperm**
can you get paid to **travel**
can you get paid to **donate blood**
can you get paid to **play video games**
can you get paid to **donate eggs**
can you get paid to **watch netflix**
can you get paid to **foster animals**

does god ever

does god ever **change his mind**
does god ever **stop pursuing us**
does god ever **change**
does god ever **speak through cats**
does god ever **sleep**
does god ever **say no**
does god ever **leave us**
does god ever **stop forgiving**
does god ever **get tired**
does god ever **want divorce**

my dad told me not to

my dad told me not to **be ashamed**
my dad told me not to **wear a bra**

my mom told me not to

my mom told me not to **waste my life**

my mom told me not to **talk to strangers**

my mom told me not to **burn trash**

my mom told me not to **put beans in my ears**

my mom told me not to **swear at school**

my mom told me not to **worry about my size**

my mom told me not to **swear**

my mom told me not to **talk to her**

my mom told me not to **drink and drive**

my mom told me not to **take acid**

do gamers

do gamers **get paid**
do gamers **wear diapers**
do gamers **have a higher iq**
do gamers **have a faster reaction time**
do gamers **have faster reflexes**
do gamers **eat bees**
do gamers **get carpal tunnel**
do gamers **make good soldiers**
do gamers **make money on youtube**
do gamers **have better reaction times**

i'm afraid to go to

i'm afraid to go to **school**
i'm afraid to go to **the doctor**
i'm afraid to go to **sleep**
i'm afraid to go to **college**
i'm afraid to go to **work**
i'm afraid to go to **the dentist**
i'm afraid to go to **therapy**
i'm afraid to go to **the gym**
i'm afraid to go to **confession**
i'm afraid to go to **the gynecologist**

my son thinks

my son thinks **i hate him**
my son thinks **i don't love him**
my son thinks **he's prince george**
my son thinks **he has adhd**
my son thinks **god's name is howard**
my son thinks **i'm mean**
my son thinks **about death**
my son thinks **everything is funny**
my son thinks **nobody likes him**
my son thinks **he has no friends**

my daughter thinks

my daughter thinks **i hate her**
my daughter thinks **i favor her sister**
my daughter thinks **everyone hates her**
my daughter thinks **she had no friends**
my daughter thinks **i don't love her**
my daughter thinks **she is better than me**
my daughter thinks **i drink too much**
my daughter thinks **she is a boy**
my daughter thinks **she is bisexual**
my daughter thinks **she is sick all the time**

does my boss

does my boss **like me**
does my boss **have aspergers**
does my boss **hate me**
does my boss **have a crush on me**
does my boss **want me to quit**
does my boss **respect me**
does my boss **trust me**
does my boss **appreciate me**
does my boss **not like me**
does my boss **value me**

should i quit

should i quit **my job**
should i quit **facebook**
should i quit **drinking**
should i quit **smoking weed**
should i quit **coffee**
should i quit **my sport**
should i quit **college**
should i quit **teaching**
should i quit **youtube**
should i quit **school**

should i go to

should i go to **law school**
should i go to **college**
should i go to **prom**
should i go to **the er**
should i go to **grad school**
should i go to **the doctor**
should i go to **medical school**
should i go to **work today**
should i go to **school today**
should i go to **the gym**

can you sell your

can you sell your **eggs**
can you sell your **blood**
can you sell your **poop**
can you sell your **soul**
can you sell your **hair**
can you sell your **uterus**
can you sell your **organs**
can you sell your **ovaries**
can you sell your **edc ticket**
can you sell your **placenta**

top ten ways to

top ten ways to **make money**
top ten ways to **fart**
top ten ways to **lose weight**
top ten ways to **save money**
top ten ways to **be a great leader**
top ten ways to **invest money**
top ten ways to **get a girlfriend**
top ten ways to **reduce stress**
top ten ways to **go to sleep**
top ten ways to **propose**

who was the first male

who was the first male **nurse**
who was the first male **model on the price is right**
who was the first male **rapper**
who was the first male **cheerleader**
who was the first male **singer**
who was the first male **ballet dancer**
who was the first male **lawyer in the united states**
who was the first male **teacher**
who was the first male **doctor**
who was the first male **covergirl**

who was the first female

who was the first female **supreme court justice**
who was the first female **cabinet member**
who was the first female **pharaoh**
who was the first female **president**
who was the first female **rapper**
who was the first female **astronaut**
who was the first female **doctor**
who was the first female **secretary of state**
who was the first female **pilot**
who was the first female **superhero**

my husband thinks i'm a

my husband thinks i'm a **liar**
my husband thinks i'm a **nag**
my husband thinks i'm a **maid**
my husband thinks i'm a **bad mother**
my husband thinks i'm a **narcissist**
my husband thinks i'm a **bad person**
my husband thinks i'm a **bad wife**
my husband thinks i'm a **gold digger**
my husband thinks i'm a **bad parent**
my husband thinks i'm a **failure**

my wife thinks i'm a

my wife thinks i'm a **loser**

my wife thinks i'm a **narcissist**

my wife thinks i'm a **bad father**

my wife thinks i'm a **liar**

my wife thinks i'm a **failure**

my wife thinks i'm a **jerk**

my wife thinks i'm a **sociopath**

my wife thinks i'm a **bad husband**

my wife thinks i'm a **bully**

my wife thinks i'm a **momma's boy**

i mistook my

i mistook my **wife for a hat**

can i perform my own

can i perform my own **title search**
can i perform my own **marriage**
can i perform my own **background check**
can i perform my own **nikah**
can i perform my own **circumcision**
can i perform my own **membrane sweep**
can i perform my own **liposuction**
can i perform my own **labiaplasty**
can i perform my own **home inspection**
can i perform my own **stretch and sweep**

what does it feel like to

what does it feel like to **die**
what does it feel like to **be high**
what does it feel like to **get shot**
what does it feel like to **be drunk**
what does it feel like to **be in love**
what does it feel like to **drown**
what does it feel like to **get stabbed**
what does it feel like to **have a stroke**
what does it feel like to **have anxiety**
what does it feel like to **be on acid**

can you die from too much

can you die from too much **water**
can you die from too much **sleep**
can you die from too much **oxygen**
can you die from too much **sex**
can you die from too much **melatonin**
can you die from too much **vitamin c**
can you die from too much **stress**
can you die from too much **protein**
can you die from too much **pain**
can you die from too much **salt**

are hot dogs made out of

are hot dogs made out of **dogs**

are hot dogs made out of **worms**

are hot dogs made out of **pig intestines**

are hot dogs made out of **rats**

are hot dogs made out of **pork**

are hot dogs made out of **chicken**

are hot dogs made out of **pigs**

are hot dogs made out of **intestines**

i'm too fat to

i'm too fat to **wipe**
i'm too fat to **eat**
i'm too fat to **date**
i'm too fat to **exercise**
i'm too fat to **lose weight**
i'm too fat to **be pretty**
i'm too fat to **be on top**
i'm too fat to **get a girlfriend**
i'm too fat to **be a hipster**
i'm too fat to **be loved**

i accidentally ate

i accidentally ate **plastic wrap**
i accidentally ate **moldy cheese**
i accidentally ate **gluten**
i accidentally ate **ants**
i accidentally ate **poop**
i accidentally ate **meat**
i accidentally ate **pork**
i accidentally ate **tin foil**
i accidentally ate **moldy bread**
i accidentally ate **undercooked chicken**

is there a real place called

is there a real place called **wakanda**

is there a real place called **kokomo**

is there a real place called **gotham**

is there a real place called **jumanji**

is there a real place called **gravity falls**

is there a real place called **dante's peak**

is there a real place called **neverland**

is there a real place called **mako island**

is there a real place called **transylvania**

is there a real place called **silent hill**

how to tell if you're a

how to tell if you're a **rebound**
how to tell if you're a **good singer**
how to tell if you're a **genius**
how to tell if you're a **hipster**
how to tell if you're a **bad person**
how to tell if you're a **good writer**
how to tell if you're a **furry**
how to tell if you're a **basic bro**
how to tell if you're a **narcissist**
how to tell if you're a **douchebag**

i flushed my

i flushed my **glasses down the toilet**
i flushed my **ring down the toilet**
i flushed my **keys down the toilet**
i flushed my **underwear down the toilet**
i flushed my **hamster down the toilet**
i flushed my **baby down the toilet**
i flushed my **phone down the toilet**
i flushed my **toothbrush down the toilet**
i flushed my **weed down the toilet**
i flushed my **dentures down the toilet**

is duct tape safe for

is duct tape safe for **fish**
is duct tape safe for **babies**
is duct tape safe for **car paint**
is duct tape safe for **skin**
is duct tape safe for **wires**
is duct tape safe for **walls**
is duct tape safe for **rats**
is duct tape safe for **electrical**
is duct tape safe for **windows**
is duct tape safe for **dogs**

i sat on

i sat on **a banana**
i sat on **my balls**
i sat on **my dog**
i sat on **my glasses**
i sat on **his lap**
i sat on **the chair**
i sat on **a throne of blood**
i sat on **gum**
i sat on **the bus**
i sat on **pee**

which is dumber

which is dumber **an idiot or a moron**

do birds

do birds **pee**
do birds **have teeth**
do birds **have ears**
do birds **fly at night**
do birds **fart**
do birds **sleep**
do birds **have tongues**
do birds **get cancer**
do birds **have a sense of smell**
do birds **eat spiders**

has a person ever been

has a person ever been **swallowed by a whale**

has a person ever been **cloned**

has a person ever been **mailed**

has a person ever been **to mars**

has a person ever been **hit by a meteor**

has a person ever been **lost in space**

has a person ever been **taxidermied**

has a person ever been **born with three eyes**

has a person ever been **born without a body**

has a person ever been **born with a tail**

why isn't anyone

why isn't anyone **ever just whelmed**
why isn't anyone **hiring me**
why isn't anyone **talking about this**
why isn't anyone **calling me for an interview**
why isn't anyone **playing battlefield 1**
why isn't anyone **talking to me**
why isn't anyone **doing anything about syria**
why isn't anyone **interested in me**
why isn't anyone **attracted to me**
why isn't anyone **allowed in antarctica**

what's it like to be

what's it like to be **married to me**
what's it like to be **blind**
what's it like to be **dead**
what's it like to be **a bat**
what's it like to be **a nurse**
what's it like to be **homeless**
what's it like to be **a flight attendant**
what's it like to be **a lawyer**
what's it like to be **happy**
what's it like to be **a girl**

how do you act like a

how do you act like a **lady**
how do you act like a **baby**
how do you act like a **princess**
how do you act like a **girlfriend**
how do you act like a **wolf**
how do you act like a **teenager**
how do you act like a **vampire**
how do you act like a **girly girl**
how do you act like a **mermaid**
how do you act like a **white girl**

why do people like

why do people like **trump**
why do people like **anime**
why do people like **rick and morty**
why do people like **horror movies**
why do people like **asmr**
why do people like **spicy food**
why do people like **sex**
why do people like **beer**
why do people like **cats**
why do people like **feet**

which is better

which is better **hmo or ppo**
which is better **lyft or uber**
which is better **iphone or android**
which is better **pubg or fortnite**
which is better **netflix or hulu**
which is better **samsung or apple**
which is better **cats or dogs**
which is better **spotify or pandora**
which is better **marvel or dc**
which is better **playstation or xbox**

rap is

rap is dead
rap is a man's soul
rap is garbage
rap is like ziti
rap is the new rock
rap is poetry
rap is bad
rap is outta control
rap is dying
rap is for morons

i didn't get the movie

i didn't get the movie **mother**
i didn't get the movie **arrival**
i didn't get the movie **interstellar**
i didn't get the movie **shutter island**
i didn't get the movie **donnie darko**
i didn't get the movie **enemy**
i didn't get the movie **split**
i didn't get the movie **logan**
i didn't get the movie **birdman**
i didn't get the movie **fight club**

movies about

movies about **watergate**

movies about **jesus**

movies about **serial killers**

movies about **depression**

movies about **mental illness**

movies about **slavery**

movies about **dogs**

movies about **time travel**

movies about **space**

movies about **magic**

tv shows about

tv shows about **college**
tv shows about **witches**
tv shows about **magic**
tv shows about **hollywood**
tv shows about **high school**
tv shows about **families**
tv shows about **time travel**
tv shows about **alaska**
tv shows about **lawyers**
tv shows about **doctors**

will it ever be possible to

will it ever be possible to **switch bodies**

will it ever be possible to **talk to animals**

will it ever be possible to **reverse aging**

will it ever be possible to **teleport**

will it ever be possible to **transfer consciousness**

will it ever be possible to **travel at the speed of light**

will it ever be possible to **go back in time**

will it ever be possible to **travel to another galaxy**

will it ever be possible to **travel faster than light**

will it ever be possible to **shrink**

can you actually buy

can you actually buy **a star**
can you actually buy **pie tops**
can you actually buy **land on mars**
can you actually buy **pizza hut shoes**
can you actually buy **a town**
can you actually buy **land on the moon**
can you actually buy **instagram followers**
can you actually buy **the bike in pokemon**
can you actually buy **an island**
can you actually buy **anything with bitcoin**

why do bad guys

why do bad guys **always win**
why do bad guys **always eat apples**
why do bad guys **always lose**
why do bad guys **always laugh**
why do bad guys **wear black**
why do bad guys **drink milk in movies**
why do bad guys **use ak 47**
why do bad guys **have red lightsabers**
why do bad guys **have english accents**
why do bad guys **laugh**

why are there so many

why are there so many **mattress stores**
why are there so many **school shootings**
why are there so many **songs about rainbows**
why are there so many **shootings**
why are there so many **pigeons in nyc**
why are there so many **ants**
why are there so many **people in china**
why are there so many **penn stations**
why are there so many **flies in my house**
why are there so many **spidermans**

why are there still

why are there still monkeys

why are there still **monkeys**
why are there still **so many jobs**
why are there still **palestinian refugees**
why are there still **floor traders**
why are there still **dry counties**
why are there still **monarchies**
why are there still **royals**
why are there still **third world countries**
why are there still **indian reservations**
why are there still **court artists**

how to get rid of your

how to get rid of your **period**
how to get rid of your **high**
how to get rid of your **double chin**
how to get rid of your **fupa**
how to get rid of your **dog**
how to get rid of your **sister**
how to get rid of your **brother**
how to get rid of your **love handles**
how to get rid of your **muffin top**
how to get rid of your **accent**

what body parts can you

what body parts can you **sell**
what body parts can you **eat**
what body parts can you **donate**
what body parts can you **live without**
what body parts can you **cup**
what body parts can you **pierce**
what body parts can you **crack**
what body parts can you **sell legally**
what body parts can you **not live without**
what body parts can you **fill with bees**

i am extremely

i am extremely **depressed**
i am extremely **cute**
i am extremely **gassy**
i am extremely **inflexible**
i am extremely **bored**
i am extremely **grateful**
i am extremely **tired**
i am extremely **sorry**
i am extremely **lonely**
i am extremely **lazy**

should i quit the

should i quit the **fire department**
should i quit the **team**
should i quit the **job i hate**
should i quit the **juul**
should i quit the **gym**
should i quit the **praise team**
should i quit the **band**
should i quit the **job i just started**
should i quit the **internet**
should i quit the **family business**

why can't

why can't **i focus**

why can't **i cry**

why can't **i pee**

why can't **i be happy**

why can't **i find a job**

why can't **i burp**

why can't **i sleep**

why can't **i eat**

why can't **i touch it**

why can't **i copy and paste**

how do you know when

how do you know when **you love someone**
how do you know when **your in love**
how do you know when **salmon is done**
how do you know when **you have the flu**
how do you know when **a mango is ripe**
how do you know when **your pregnant**
how do you know when **a guy likes you**
how do you know when **you are in ketosis**
how do you know when **easter is**
how do you know when **you are uncomfortable in cyberspace**

i cheated on my boyfriend with

i cheated on my boyfriend with **his best friend**
i cheated on my boyfriend with **a girl**
i cheated on my boyfriend with **my boss**
i cheated on my boyfriend with **his sister**
i cheated on my boyfriend with **a woman**
i cheated on my boyfriend with **his dad**
i cheated on my boyfriend with **my friend**
i cheated on my boyfriend with **my ex**
i cheated on my boyfriend with **my best friend**
i cheated on my boyfriend with **my brother**

i cheated on my girlfriend with

i cheated on my girlfriend with **my ex**
i cheated on my girlfriend with **my friend**
i cheated on my girlfriend with **a guy**
i cheated on my girlfriend with **my best friend**
i cheated on my girlfriend with **a prostitute**
i cheated on my girlfriend with **her sister**
i cheated on my girlfriend with **her brother**
i cheated on my girlfriend with **a gay guy**
i cheated on my girlfriend with **my ex wife**
i cheated on my girlfriend with **her friend**

i did the macarena

i did the macarena **with a homeless guy in an elevator**

is it cool to

is it cool to **vape**

is it cool to **be a nerd**

is it cool to **wear a watch**

is it cool to **smoke**

is it cool to **be hip**

is it cool to **wear a fanny pack**

is it cool to **wear socks with sandals**

is it cool to **dab**

is it cool to **be an introvert**

is it cool to **say cool**

why am i afraid of

why am i afraid of **the dark**
why am i afraid of **love**
why am i afraid of **clowns**
why am i afraid of **heights**
why am i afraid of **spiders**
why am i afraid of **death**
why am i afraid of **success**
why am i afraid of **needles**
why am i afraid of **cats**
why am i afraid of **everything**

is it lame to

is it lame to **go out by yourself**
is it lame to **go to a bar alone**
is it lame to **go to a concert by yourself**
is it lame to **wear fake glasses**
is it lame to **travel alone**
is it lame to **go to the movies by yourself**
is it lame to **wear a helmet**
is it lame to **use tinder**
is it lame to **propose on valentine's day**
is it lame to **go to a concert with your mom**

someone called me

someone called me a **square**
someone called me a **puppy**
someone called me a **goat**
someone called me a **snake**
someone called me a **unicorn**
someone called me a **snack**
someone called me a **loser**
someone called me a **ginger**
someone called me a **tool**
someone called me a **liar**

redheads are

redheads are **superheroes**

redheads are **going extinct**

redheads are **mutants**

redheads are **unicorns**

redheads are **genetic superheroes**

redheads are **crazy**

redheads are **smarter**

redheads are **mean**

redheads are **irish**

redheads are **witches**

still sad about

still sad about **mcr**
still sad about **miscarriage**
still sad about **break up**
still sad about **dogs death**
still sad about **my ex**
still sad about **my divorce**
still sad about **prince**
still sad about **election**
still sad about **bowie**
still sad about **first love**

why do i get sad when

why do i get sad when **my boyfriend leaves**
why do i get sad when **it rains**
why do i get sad when **i smoke weed**
why do i get sad when **i'm alone**
why do i get sad when **i'm tired**
why do i get sad when **i'm on my period**
why do i get sad when **i eat**
why do i get sad when **the sun goes down**
why do i get sad when **i finish a tv series**
why do i get sad when **i see babies**

why do i get excited when

why do i get excited when **i see him**
why do i get excited when **i see my crush**
why do i get excited when **bad things happen**
why do i get excited when **i have to poop**
why do i get excited when **it rains**
why do i get excited when **he texts me**
why do i get excited when **i see blood**
why do i get excited when **i see my ex**

how do you pretend to be

how do you pretend to be **a virgin**
how do you pretend to be **high**
how do you pretend to be **sick**
how do you pretend to be **happy**
how do you pretend to be **confident**
how do you pretend to be **a carrot**
how do you pretend to be **pregnant**
how do you pretend to be **offline on facebook**
how do you pretend to be **drunk**
how do you pretend to be **asleep**

my friends are all

my friends are all **fake**
my friends are all **dead**
my friends are all **heathens**
my friends are all **losers**
my friends arc all **in relationshlps**
my friends are all **depressed**
my friends are all **prettier than me**
my friends are all **older than me**
my friends are all **selfish**
my friends are all **gone**

should i tell my girlfriend

should i tell my girlfriend **i cheated on her**
should i tell my girlfriend **i miss her**
should i tell my girlfriend **i kissed another girl**
should i tell my girlfriend **everything**
should i tell my girlfriend **i'm bi**
should i tell my girlfriend **i have aspergers**
should i tell my girlfriend **i have hpv**
should i tell my girlfriend **i have herpes**
should i tell my girlfriend **how much i make**
should i tell my girlfriend **i cheated on my ex**

should i tell my boyfriend

should i tell my boyfriend **i cheated on him**
should i tell my boyfriend **i love him**
should i tell my boyfriend **i have hpv**
should i tell my boyfriend **about my past**
should i tell my boyfriend **everything**
should i tell my boyfriend **i snooped**
should i tell my boyfriend **i have a uti**
should i tell my boyfriend **i cuddled with another guy**
should i tell my boyfriend **i'm pregnant**
should i tell my boyfriend **i had plastic surgery**

who was the first person in the world to

who was the first person in the world to **fart**

#

why do i feel so

why do i feel so **tired**
why do i feel so **alone**
why do i feel so **bloated**
why do i feel so **lonely**
why do i feel so **sad**
why do i feel so **empty**
why do i feel so **depressed**
why do i feel so **weak**
why do i feel so **nauseous**
why do i feel so **dizzy**

can robots

can robots **have feelings**
can robots **fly**
can robots **love**
can robots **take over the world**
can robots **be creative**
can robots **become self aware**
can robots **feel pain**
can robots **smell**
can robots **eat**
can robots **have babies**

am i too fat for

am i too fat for **him**
am i too fat for **yoga**
am i too fat for **orangetheory**
am i too fat for **a bikini**
am i too fat for **disney world rides**
am i too fat for **a tummy tuck**
am i too fat for **roller coasters**
am i too fat for **love**
am i too fat for **ballet**
am i too fat for **shorts**

am i too skinny for

am i too skinny for **a bbl**
am i too skinny for **a guy**
am i too skinny for **my height**
am i too skinny for **the army**
am i too skinny for **fat transfer**
am i too skinny for **breast implants**
am i too skinny for **liposuction**
am i too skinny for **a girl**
am i too skinny for **a tattoo**
am i too skinny for **a belly button piercing**

i swallowed a

i swallowed a **fly**
i swallowed a **bug**
i swallowed a **sword i levitated**
i swallowed a **bone**
i swallowed a **penny**
i swallowed a **piece of plastic**
i swallowed a **tonsil stone**
i swallowed a **cherry pit**
i swallowed a **bee**
i swallowed a **toothpick**

i think i accidentally

i think i accidentally **ate mold**
i think i accidentally **ran a red light**
i think i accidentally **deleted my instagram**
i think i accidentally **sold my soul**
i think i accidentally **swallowed glass**
i think i accidentally **put two tampons in**
i think i accidentally **plagiarized**
i think i accidentally **downloaded a virus**
i think i accidentally **deleted an app**
i think i accidentally **ate raw chicken**

google are you

google are you **connected to the cia**
google are you **there**
google are you **stupid**
google are you **my friend**
google are you **gay**
google are you **a boy or a girl**
google are you **listening**
google are you **better than siri**
google are you **smart**
google are you **real**

why don't i like

why don't i like **people**
why don't i like **myself**
why don't i like **water**
why don't i like **kids**
why don't i like **my family**
why don't i like **beer**
why don't i like **hugs**
why don't i like **avocado**
why don't i like **sex**
why don't i like **coffee**

my dad wants me to be

my dad wants me to be **a doctor**
my dad wants me to be **like him**
my dad wants me to be **a lawyer**
my dad wants me to be **perfect**
my dad wants me to be **an engineer**
my dad wants me to be **fat**
my dad wants me to be **more manly**
my dad wants me to be **a boy**
my dad wants me to be **straight**

my mom wants me to be

my mom wants me to be **a girl**
my mom wants me to be **girly**
my mom wants me to be **perfect**
my mom wants me to be **like her**
my mom wants me to be **a doctor**
my mom wants me to be **more feminine**
my mom wants me to be **someone i'm not**
my mom wants me to be **a doctor but i don't**
my mom wants me to be **just like her**
my mom wants me to be **religious**

why does jesus have

why does jesus have **a last name**
why does jesus have **to die**
why does jesus have **abs**
why does jesus have **a tomb**
why does jesus have **a tattoo**
why does jesus have **two fingers up**
why does jesus have **white hair in revelation**
why does jesus have **two different genealogies**
why does jesus have **half brothers**
why does jesus have **a spanish name**

my eyes look

my eyes look **tired**
my eyes look **dead**
my eyes look **yellow**
my eyes look **different**
my eyes look **black**
my eyes look **weird**
my eyes look **sad**
my eyes look **droopy**
my eyes look **old**
my eyes look **glassy**

can a woman

can a woman **get pregnant at 48**
can a woman **be a pastor**
can a woman **take viagra**
can a woman **be knighted**
can a woman **be a navy seal**
can a woman **be a deacon**
can a woman **be a priest**
can a woman **get a hernia**
can a woman **be a rabbi**
can a woman **get a uti from a man**

can a man

can a man **get pregnant**

can a man **get a uti**

can a man **be a widow**

can a man **lactate**

can a man **be tested for hpv**

can a man **get bv**

can a man **give a woman a uti**

can a man **catch a yeast infection**

can a man **give birth**

can a man **give you bv**

my feet smell like

my feet smell like **weed**
my feet smell like **cheese**
my feet smell like **popcorn**
my feet smell like **vinegar**
my feet smell like **corn chips**
my feet smell like **death**
my feet smell like **doritos**
my feet smell like **butter**
my feet smell like **yeast**
my feet smell like **wet dog**

what happens if you drink

what happens if you drink **too much water**
what happens if you drink **pee**
what happens if you drink **too much milk**
what happens if you drink **expired milk**
what happens if you drink **blood**
what happens if you drink **salt water**
what happens if you drink **expired beer**
what happens if you drink **bad wine**
what happens if you drink **gasoline**
what happens if you drink **too much coffee**

why do americans

why do americans **work so much**

why do americans **celebrate cinco de mayo**

why do americans **drive on the right**

why do americans **love guns**

why do americans **call it soccer**

why do americans **celebrate thanksgiving**

why do americans **tip**

why do americans **eat so much**

why do americans **pay taxes**

why do americans **say zee**

my mom eats

my mom eats **too much**

my mom eats **all my food**

my mom eats **so unhealthy**

my mom eats **too much junk food**

my mom eats **too loud**

my mom eats **so much**

my mom eats **so loud**

my mom eats **a lot**

my mom eats **expired food**

my dad eats

my dad eats **pasta in spanish**
my dad eats **too much**
my dad eats **like a pig**
my dad eats **sugar with his nose**
my dad eats **everything in the house**
my dad eats **unhealthy**
my dad eats **so loud**
my dad eats **smoke from a gatorade bottle**
my dad eats **all the food**
my dad eats **poop**

chocolate flavored

chocolate flavored **gum**
chocolate flavored **cigars**
chocolate flavored **toothpaste**
chocolate flavored **alcohol**
chocolate flavored **wine**
chocolate flavored **vodka**
chocolate flavored **beer**
chocolate flavored **condoms**
chocolate flavored **water**
chocolate flavored **whiskey**

why are the french so

why are the french so **thin**
why are the french so **romantic**
why are the french so **bad at war**
why are the french so **short**
why are the french so **bad at english**
why are the french so **cool**
why are the french so **good at maths**
why are the french so **difficult**
why are the french so **miserable**
why are the french so **stuck up**

why are the english

why are the english **called limes**
why are the english **called tommies**
why are the english **called poms**
why are the english **so snobby**
why are the english **so reserved**
why are the english **obsessed with tea**
why are the english **such bastards**
why are the english **so cold**
why are the english **police called bobbies**
why are the english **royal family german**

why do comedians

why do comedians **sweat so much**

why do comedians **wear all black**

why do comedians **sit in the back**

why do comedians **wear leather**

why do comedians **get depressed**

why do comedians **end so abruptly**

why do comedians **become comedians**

why do comedians **kill themselves**

why do comedians **die young**

why do comedians **have a stool**

do fish know

do fish know **they are wet**
do fish know **when it is christmas**
do fish know **they are in water**
do fish know **their name**
do fish know **who their owner is**
do fish know **when they are full**
do fish know **they are alive**
do fish know **when it's raining**
do fish know **their name**
do fish know **they are fish**

do dogs

do dogs **dream**
do dogs **sweat**
do dogs **go to heaven**
do dogs **see color**
do dogs **cry**
do dogs **get colds**
do dogs **like hugs**
do dogs **have periods**
do dogs **smile**
do dogs **have souls**

do cats

do cats **fart**
do cats **see color**
do cats **get colds**
do cats **dream**
do cats **sweat**
do cats **cry**
do cats **eat mice**
do cats **have periods**
do cats **blink**
do cats **have nine lives**

what happens if you google

what happens if you google **google**
what happens if you google **your social security number**
what happens if you google **your name**
what happens if you google **8766**
what happens if you google **bomb instructions**
what happens if you google **your name at 3am**
what happens if you google **google 99 times**
what happens if you google **something illegal**
what happens if you google **yourself**
what happens if you google **tiananmen square in china**

will someone ever invent

will someone ever invent **a time machine**

why is my girlfriend so

why is my girlfriend so **cute**

why is my girlfriend so **beautiful**

why is my girlfriend so **mean**

why is my girlfriend so **hot**

why is my girlfriend so **crazy**

why is my girlfriend so **dumb**

why is my girlfriend so **annoying**

why is my girlfriend so **weird**

why is my girlfriend so **stupid**

why is my girlfriend so **emotional**

why is my boyfriend so

why is my boyfriend so **cute**

why is my boyfriend so **mean**

why is my boyfriend so **jealous**

why is my boyfriend so **hot**

why is my boyfriend so **clingy**

why is my boyfriend so **weird**

why is my boyfriend so **insecure**

why is my boyfriend so **selfish**

why is my boyfriend so **dumb**

why is my boyfriend so **immature**

are there still

are there still **slaves**
are there still **pirates**
are there still **world fairs**
are there still **chat rooms**
are there still **rajneesh**
are there still **circuses**
are there still **paperboys**
are there still **orphanages in the us**
are there still **troops in iraq**
are there still **sannyasins**

would jesus

would jesus **wear a rolex**
would jesus **carry a gun**
would jesus **pull the switch**
would jesus **have a gun**
would jesus **have long hair**
would jesus **be vegan**
would jesus **be a capitalist**
would jesus **forgive judas**

does the bible say not to

does the bible say not to **cuss**
does the bible say not to **drink**
does the bible say not to **eat meat**
does the bible say not to **judge**
does the bible say not to **gamble**
does the bible say not to **cut your hair**
does the bible say not to **have sex before marriage**
does the bible say not to **smoke weed**
does the bible say not to **get tattoos**
does the bible say not to **mix races**

what's a word that means

what's a word that means **never give up**
what's a word that means **good and bad**
what's a word that means **more than love**
what's a word that means **deep in thought**
what's a word that means **you don't care**
what's a word that means **more than perfect**
what's a word that means **happy and sad**
what's a word that means **not giving up**
what's a word that means **someone is easy to manipulate**
what's a word that means **more than happy**

should i tell my son

should i tell my son **to fight back**
should i tell my son **he has adhd**
should i tell my son **he has autism**
should i tell my son **i don't like his girlfriend**
should i tell my son **he has aspergers**
should i tell my son **his dad is in jail**
should i tell my son **who his real father is**
should i tell my son **to hit back**
should i tell my son **his girlfriend is cheating**
should i tell my son **there is no santa**

should i tell my daughter

should i tell my daughter **her boyfriend is cheating**
should i tell my daughter **her husband is cheating**
should i tell my daughter **she is overweight**
should i tell my daughter **i don't like her boyfriend**
should i tell my daughter **she is beautiful**
should i tell my daughter **i read her diary**
should i tell my daughter **she has autism**
should i tell my daughter **her dad cheated**
should i tell my daughter **she has a half sister**
should i tell my daughter **she's adopted**

is it healthy to eat

is it healthy to eat **your boogers**
is it healthy to eat **tuna everyday**
is it healthy to eat **the skin of salmon**
is it healthy to eat **meat**
is it healthy to eat **raw eggs**
is it healthy to eat **shrimp**
is it healthy to eat **1000 calories a day**
is it healthy to eat **snow**
is it healthy to eat **liver**
is it healthy to eat **paper**

i'm ready to give up on

i'm ready to give up on **everything**

i'm ready to give up on **life**

i'm ready to give up on **my relationship**

i'm ready to give up on **my marriage**

i'm ready to give up on **love**

i'm ready to give up on **breastfeeding**

i'm ready to give up on **dating**

i'm ready to give up on **my dog**

how to describe

how to describe **yourself**

how to describe **love**

how to describe **pain**

how to describe **a voice**

how to describe **music**

how to describe **melody**

how to describe **a smile**

how to describe **someone**

how to describe **skin color**

how to describe **anxiety**

nicer way to say

nicer way to say **stupid**
nicer way to say **fat**
nicer way to say **asap**
nicer way to say **poor**
nicer way to say **fired**
nicer way to say **half assed**
nicer way to say **old**
nicer way to say **dumb**
nicer way to say **homeless**
nicer way to say **ignorant**

what is a

what is a **coat of arms**
what is a **good credit score**
what is a **polygon**
what is a **verb**
what is a **thesis**
what is a **metaphor**
what is a **pronoun**
what is a **prime number**
what is a **simile**
what is a **meme**

what would happen if i

what would happen if i **died**
what would happen if i **touched lava**
what would happen if i **ate myself**
what would happen if i **stopped talking**
what would happen if i **only ate eggs**
what would happen if i **drank gasoline**
what would happen if i **walked out of school**
what would happen if i **injected myself with water**
what would happen if i **ate weed**
what would happen if i **ran away**

what would happen if someone

what would happen if someone **received the wrong blood type**
what would happen if someone **had faulty spindle fibers**
what would happen if someone **tried to escape**
what would happen if someone **fell into lava**
what would happen if someone **punched the president**
what would happen if someone **used 100 percent of their brain**
what would happen if someone **traveled at the speed of light**
what would happen if someone **was born in space**
what would happen if someone **detonated a nuclear bomb today**
what would happen if someone **ate poop**

why do people

why do people **yawn**
why do people **snore**
why do people **cheat**
why do people **lie**
why do people **smoke**
why do people **stutter**
why do people **bully**
why do people **fart**
why do people **sneeze**
why do people **cry**

why do people say

why do people say **bless you**
why do people say **xmas**
why do people say **merry chrysler**
why do people say **break a leg**
why do people say **bet**
why do people say **oof**
why do people say **like so much**
why do people say **geronimo**
why do people say **uncle**
why do people say **um**

why do they call it

why do they call it **indian summer**
why do they call it **the clap**
why do they call it **french kissing**
why do they call it **a funny bone**
why do they call it **420**
why do they call it **the big apple**
why do they call it **catfishing**
why do they call it **the dead sea**
why do they call it **a charlie horse**
why do they call it **the birds and the bees**

is it possible to

is it possible to **be allergic to water**
is it possible to **learn this power**
is it possible to **live without a spine**
is it possible to **fly**
is it possible to **have black hair**
is it possible to **go back in time**
is it possible to **be allergic to weed**
is it possible to **time travel**
is it possible to **live on mars**
is it possible to **get shorter**

i had a dream i was

i had a dream i was **pregnant**
i had a dream i was **7**
i had a dream i was **shot**
i had a dream i was **getting married**
i had a dream i was **kidnapped**
i had a dream i was **being chased**
i had a dream i was **in jail**
i had a dream i was **dying**
i had a dream i was **flying**
i had a dream i was **a muffler**

whats the song that goes

whats the song that goes **la la la la**
whats the song that goes **shoo shoo**
whats the song that goes **boom boom boom**
whats the song that goes **bum bum bum**
whats the song that goes **you and you**
whats the song that goes **duh duh duh**
whats the song that goes **dun dun dun**
whats the song that goes **skrt skrt**
whats the song that goes **dudududu dudududu**
whats the song that goes **and iiii**

do my parents know

do my parents know **i smoke weed**
do my parents know **me**
do my parents know **i fap**
do my parents know **what i do on the internet**
do my parents know **what i search**
do my parents know **i'm gay**
do my parents know **i'm sexually active**
do my parents know **i'm high**
do my parents know **i smoke cigarettes**
do my parents know **i drink**

why do men

why do men **have nipples**
why do men **lie**
why do men **go bald**
why do men **have facial hair**
why do men **snore**
why do men **get boners**
why do men **wear ties**
why do men **like sex**
why do men **like feet**
why do men **ghost**

why do women

why do women **wear hijab**
why do women **wear thongs**
why do women **wear makeup**
why do women **have periods**
why do women **wear bras**
why do women **wear high heels**
why do women **miscarry**
why do women **get cramps**
why do women **douche**
why do women **talk so much**

can a dead person

can a dead person **ejaculate**
can a dead person **fart**
can a dead person **come back to life**
can a dead person **be libeled**
can a dead person **hear**
can a dead person **open their eyes**
can a dead person **cry**
can a dead person **call you**
can a dead person **donate blood**
can a dead person **give birth**

when you die you

when you die you **die**

when you die you **become a star**

when you die you **become a tree**

when you die you **go to heaven**

when you die you **lose 21 grams**

when you die you **wake up**

when you die you **are born again**

when you die you **know you're dead**

when you die you **will meet god**

when you die you **poop**

stop finishing my sentences

stop finishing my sentences **google**